KTG know the game

Sailing

produced in collaboration with the
Royal Yachting Association

CONTENTS

FOREWORD

When you pick up this book to glance at it, you will show that you are interested in sailing. Whilst it gives you the essential facts about boats and their equipment, and why they move at all, it is not my purpose to make you feel expert enough to venture forth in any weather on any sea. Like most sports, there is an element of danger. Here in these pages, you are introduced to the 'How and Why' and some of the rules.

Every time you venture forth in a sailing boat, you will learn something new. You will learn to feel part of the boat, riding the waves together. Until you do, you are not really a sailor.

Having read this book you will, I hope, read many others on sailing, its history, perhaps, or its development and organisation.

I would not want you to feel that you must learn from this book only. There are many organisations, affiliated to the Royal Yachting Association: clubs, schools, teaching establishments and Sailing Centres all waiting to teach and help you enjoy our sport.

The Royal Yachting Association and the National School Sailing Association run a National scheme of Proficiency. The Elementary Certificate is the first step. You should also become a member of a club and the R.Y.A. to obtain all the information, booklets etc. which will help you learn more.

For your own personal safety, and that of your family, if you have one, it is wise to learn properly.

In these pages you will read that it is imprudent to venture forth without warm clothing, oilskins and a lifejacket or buoyancy aid. You will read that you should take not only yourself and your friends or family but an anchor, a bailer or bucket, a paddle or oars and rowlocks (in case the wind drops) and, if you are going to sail on the sea, some flares, red for distress, white for attracting attention. You will read these words and think 'What is all the fuss about?'

My answer is very simple. 'It may never happen, especially to me' is one of the old, old remarks which, after a bit of experience, we all know to be foolish. But don't think that the sport is unduly dangerous. It isn't if you know what you are doing.

If you have many questions to ask after reading this book, I shall not be the least surprised. I and my colleagues at the Royal Yachting Association will be happy to try to answer them, or to put you in touch with somebody who will help you to enjoy a sport which we all think is second to none.

GORDON FAIRLEY,
Royal Yachting Association,
Woking, Surrey.

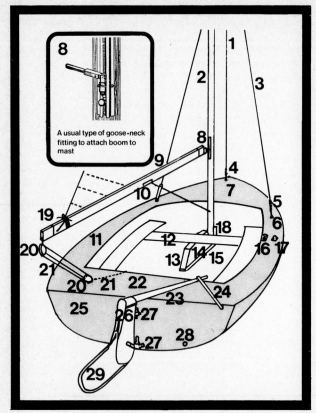

A usual type of goose-neck fitting to attach boom to mast

Fig. 1

Parts of the boat

1. Forestay (attached to the bow by a shackle)
2. Mast
3. Shroud (made of wire)
4. Jib tack strop (see 'Rigging your boat')
5. Adjustable rigging screws (or lanyard)
6. Chainplate (secure point for rigging)
7. Foredeck
8. Goose-neck (see inset diagram)
9. Boom
10. Kicking strap (to hold boom down)
11. Side deck
12. Thwart (a seat across the boat)
13. Centre board case
14. Toestraps (as support when 'sitting out')
15. Bottom boards
16. Jamb cleat (to trap jib sheet)
17. Fairlead (a ring to alter direction of jib sheet)
18. Mast step
19. Mainsail clew outhaul (rope to 'stretch' sail aft)
20. Mainsheet blocks (which you know on land as pulleys)
21. Mainsheet (to pull in or let out mainsail and boom)
22. After-deck (the back end is called the 'after-end')
23. Tiller (for turning the rudder)
24. Tiller extension (used when 'sitting out')
25. Transom (or stern, as opposed to the bow of the boat)
26. Rudder stock
27. Rudder pintles and gudgeons (the rudder is removable)
28. Drain hole (sometimes flaps, but both to let water **out**)
29. Rudder blade (which is 'liftable')

The boat's main controls

Every part of the boat, its ropes and sails, has a special name. The ropes which pull the sails UP are called **halyards.** The ropes to pull the sails IN, or let them OUT, are called **sheets.** The other controls are the **tiller,** which you hold to turn the **rudder,** and the **centreboard** (a movable keel which is adjusted to keep your boat from 'skidding' across the water).

Fig. 1 illustrates many other names which will eventually form part of your sailing vocabulary. Fig. 2 illustrates the names of the parts of the sails and equipment not actually in the boat itself.

The shrouds (Fig. 1 item 3) are adjustable by various methods in different boats. They may be tensioned or slackened to better the stability of the sail plan.

Your boat must float

Because of the ease with which sailing dinghies can capsize, they are all built with water-tight compartments under seats, after-deck or fore-deck, or supplied with strong air bags to fit in similar places. This in-built buoyancy is vital to your safety. The well-built dinghy will have sufficient to hold up the boat, its two-man crew and plenty of buoyancy in reserve.

Additionally, many are fitted with 'self-bailers' which are operated by suction at low speeds. They will open and release water which is lying in the boat. Alternatively you must keep the boat dry by using a scoop-bailer or bucket which should always be on board.

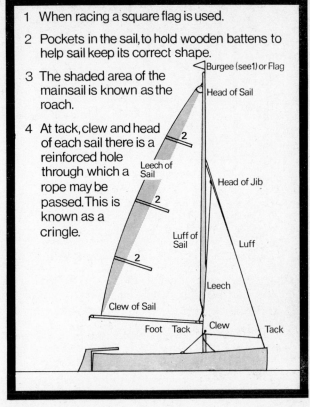

1 When racing a square flag is used.

2 Pockets in the sail, to hold wooden battens to help sail keep its correct shape.

3 The shaded area of the mainsail is known as the roach.

4 At tack, clew and head of each sail there is a reinforced hole through which a rope may be passed. This is known as a cringle.

Burgee (see 1) or Flag
Head of Sail
Leech of Sail
Head of Jib
Luff of Sail
Luff
Leech
Clew of Sail
Foot   Tack   Clew   Tack

Fig. 2

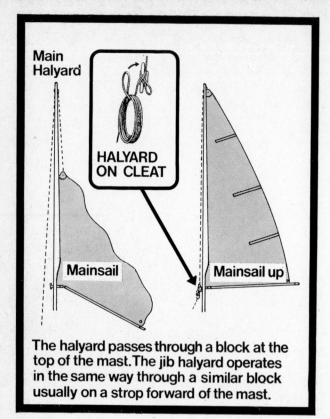

Main
Halyard

HALYARD
ON CLEAT

Mainsail

Mainsail up

The halyard passes through a block at the top of the mast. The jib halyard operates in the same way through a similar block usually on a strop forward of the mast.

Fig. 3

CONTROLLING YOUR BOAT

The Halyards

In a dinghy, with fore and aft 'Burmudan' sails, there are two halyards—one for hoisting the main and one for hoisting the jib. In Fig. 3 you will see how the main halyard works. It is 'reeved' through a 'block' at the top of the mast and, when the sail is pulled up, is secured on a cleat at or near the foot of the mast. The jib halyard works in a similar way for the jib.

The Sheets

Whichever side the boom is on, the mainsheet serves to haul in or let out the sail. The jib is controlled by a sheet on each side of the boat, and the appropriate one is used. When your boat is facing dead into the wind the sails will not fill, whatever you do. Boat I in Fig. 4 is said to be 'in irons.' Boat S, with the wind on the starboard side, is on starboard tack. Boat P is on port tack. They are both 'close-hauled' (the sheets are pulled in as close as they can be). Boats X, Y and Z show the other attitudes in which you can put your boat. X's helmsman has 'eased his sheets' and the boat is 'reaching' (across the wind). Y is 'broad reaching' and Z 'running before'—her sails wide open like an umbrella.

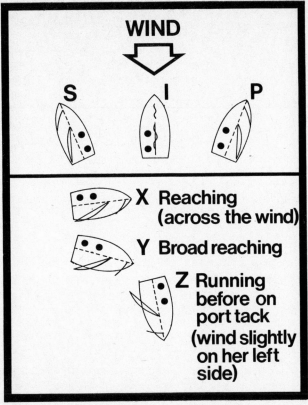

Fig. 4

The Rudder

Notice that the crew in Fig. 4 always sit on the side of the boat nearest the wind. Therefore, it is true to say that, if the helmsman pulls the tiller towards him, the boat will turn away from the wind. So, if he pushes the tiller away from him, she will turn into the wind. ALWAYS sit with your back to the wind on the windy side. This helps to keep the boat upright, like leaning over on a bicycle.

The Centreboard

Boats S and P have got their centreboard fully down, otherwise they would slide across the water, crab-wise. X doesn't have so much wind pressure in her sails, so the centreboard would be half-way down. Z is in no danger of 'skidding' and should have hardly any centreboard down, since it DOES act to slow the boat up a bit and, unless it is needed should be adjusted as described.

Stopping your boat

Suppose that you are sailing Boat P, and want to stop. LET EVERYTHING GO. Let go the mainsheet, your crew releases the jib sheet and you let go of the tiller. The boat's natural tendency will be to turn up into the wind and the sails will 'weathercock' and not fill. She will be 'in irons' as it were. This is the basic safety position. If you are driving the boat too hard, and your combined weights are insufficient to keep her upright, or there is a SUDDEN gust of wind, don't cling on to the mainsheet in fear! Just let it go and the boat will 'recover'.

PREPARING TO GO AFLOAT

It will often be necessary to hoist the sails whilst the boat is actually in the water but it is preferable to get everything ready to hoist whilst still on the shore. Standing up in a wobbling boat reaps its own reward!

Let us assume that you have chosen a launching site where the wind is blowing off the shore. With your boat still on its trolley:—

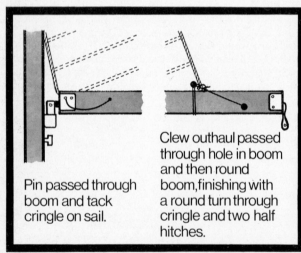

Pin passed through boom and tack cringle on sail.

Clew outhaul passed through hole in boom and then round boom, finishing with a round turn through cringle and two half hitches.

Fig. 5

Rigging the sails

1. Put in your sail battens—the correct size into the correct pocket, thin end first, if the battens are tapered.

2. Take the clew of the mainsail and lead the footrope or slides from the FRONT end of the boom into the groove on the boom until the tack cringle comes opposite its attachment at the front end of the boom. (Have a look at Fig. 2 again.) Push the tack pin through the boom and the tack cringle; then tension the sail by pulling the clew end out along the boom and tying it as illustrated in Fig. 5 always tying round the boom and finishing with a round turn through the cringle and two half hitches. (See page 30.)

3. Now take the tack of the jib sail and secure it to the jib tack strop, with the shackle provided. All the way up the luff of the jib you will find clips (properly called 'hanks'). Hank these on to the forestay wire. SEE THAT YOU DO NOT TWIST THE SAIL. Attach the jib halyard and see that it is not twisted round the forestay.

Running rigging

4. Now sort out the jib sheets and mainsheet. Pass the jib sheets through the fairlead on each side of the boat and tie a Figure of eight knot in the end of each. Then make sure that the mainsheet passes correctly through its blocks and that there is a Figure of eight knot in the end of it, as well. (See page 29 for knots.)

5. Hoist your burgee on its own halyard. (On many dinghies the burgee remains permanently fixed at the masthead.)

Plate 1. Preparing the boat on shore.

Plate 2. Crew holding boat head to wind with sheets free.

Plate 3. Two trainee crews ready for the 'off'.

Into the water

6. Push the trolley into the water, KEEPING THE BOW OF THE BOAT POINTING INTO THE WIND, and float the boat off, holding on to it. (See Plates 1, 2 and 3.)

7. The crew holds the bow and the helmsman slackens off the goose-neck slide, inserts the boom on to it and, **being careful not to twist the mainsail,** inserts the luff-rope or slides into the groove on the mast. He shackles the main halyard to the mainsail and hauls it gently up the mast. He should make sure that the sail is *fully* up. Then he secures the halyard on the cleat and hauls the jib up, securing its halyard onto the other cleat.

8. Both crew keep the head of the boat into the wind, leaving the sails loose and all sheets free. The helmsman puts in the RUDDER (vital equipment!) with its folding blade fully in the 'up' position.

9. Attach the 'kicking strap', which leads from the boom to the foot of the mast, and holds the boom down.

10. Finally check that you have life-jackets, oilskins, an anchor and flares (if on the sea) and that the centreboard is free.

9

Reefing for safety

It is possible in many dinghies to reduce the area of sail if the weather is really blowing. As a beginner, you should not venture forth at all but, when you are experienced, you can reef a boat with a sliding goose-neck as follows. Turn it into the wind, preferably on a mooring or the shore. Slacken off the goose-neck 'lock', and ease the main halyard. Take the boom partly out of the goose-neck fitting and roll the required amount of sail round the boom, pulling it out towards the end of the boom, so that it rolls neatly. Replace the boom, haul up the sail, tighten the goose-neck 'lock'. (Fig. 6.)

If in doubt about the weather, REEF before going afloat.

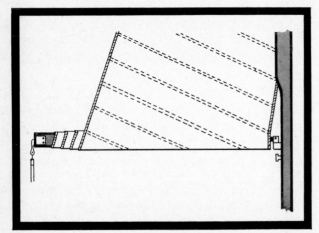

Fig. 6

GOING AFLOAT

We have described the preparation for going afloat from a weather shore (i.e., one where the wind is blowing off the land). It is vastly preferably to launch from a weather shore. However, it is not always possible and launching must sometimes take place from a lee shore (i.e., one where the wind is blowing ON TO the land).

In Fig. 7 launching from a weather shore takes place as follows:—

1. The crew holds the bow of the boat into the wind.

2. The helmsman prepares the boat.

3. The boat can be turned either way and she will tend to blow away from the shore, even before the sails are 'sheeted in'.

Now look at the lee shore picture (Fig. 8). In the first place you have to rig your boat and hoist the sails with the bow pointing into the wind, so the crew has to stand in deeper water. When you are ready to set off, the helmsman has to hold the boat by the stern, whilst the crew gets aboard. Then the helmsman has to shove off and leap into the boat. Note that, in this case, there is little choice about direction. It would be mad to try to turn towards the tree, because it is VITAL to get the centreboard down a bit, otherwise the boat will drift back on to the land. Also, it is far more difficult to get the rudder down quickly and, again, this makes it less certain that you will get away from the shore when launching from a lee shore.

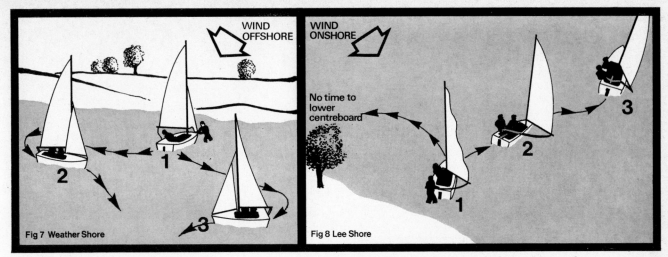

Fig 7 Weather Shore

Fig 8 Lee Shore

1. Crew holds bow of boat into wind.
2. Helmsman prepares the boat.
3. The boat can be turned either way and she will blow away from shore.

1. Helmsman holds bow of boat into wind, crew sorts out boat.
2. After a good shove, helmsman gets in and lowers rudder, sheets in sail and crew carefully lowers centreboard.
3. Both main and jib sheeted in, centreboard fully down.

We have taken the two extreme examples of the wind blowing off the shore (weather shore) and the wind blowing on to the shore (lee shore). There are many occasions when you will find the wind blowing **along** the shore. Clearly, then, you carry out the same drill. Point the bow into the wind, rig the boat and then launch her on the line which will take you quickly away from the shore.

By now, you will have realised that the centreboard and rudder are **very** vital pieces of equipment. They must be brought into use as soon as possible. However, if the crew member is too quick in lowering the centreboard, the whole operation will come to a grinding halt. Therefore, in the lee shore illustration, position 2 is shown as a 'reaching' situation, where only half the centreboard is down.

11

Handling the boat

As soon as you have got afloat, you will be well advised to 'make passage' across the wind. On a 'reach', it is not difficult to control the boat and you will gradually become familiar with the feel of it. Basically both the crew should, as we have said before, sit with their backs to the wind. The helmsman should always sit with his front foot forward, with the mainsheet in his front hand and the tiller held in the hand nearest the stern. The crew sits alongside him, nearer the bow, with the opposite jib sheet in his hand.

If the helmsman wishes to pull the mainsheet in, it will be necessary to pull it in as far as possible with one hand, then trap the mainsheet with the thumb of the hand on the tiller, shift his mainsheet hand up the rope and 'repeat' as often as necessary. Fig. 9 shows how the tiller hand should be, and the 'trapping' action when sheeting in.

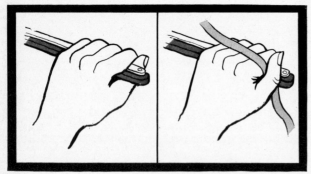

Fig. 9 Grasping   *Trapping*

Going about

Sooner or later, wherever you are sailing, you will have to turn the boat through the wind and get her on to the other 'tack' so that you can go back the other way or progress towards your 'destination'.

With his front foot forward and the leg nearest the stern tucked in seemingly 'under the seat', the helmsman is poised to 'go through the drill' of going about.

The sequence should be smoothly executed but is taught, in the R.Y.A. method, as a series of 'by numbers' tasks. It can be practised on land with two chairs opposite each other, a broom stick and a piece of old rope!

1. Check 'ready to go about'—all ropes etc.
2. Look all round to see that no other boat is close.
3. Helmsman, when ready, calls out 'ready about'.
4. Crew checks all round boat for any obstructions.
5. Helmsman transfers the mainsheet to his 'back' hand (holding both tiller and mainsheet in one hand), he then calls 'lee oh!' and pushes the tiller AWAY from him.
6. Crew releases jib sheet and picks up the other one.
7. Crew balances boat as it comes upright.
8. Boat is still turning into the wind.
9. Boom will start to come in towards the centre of the boat.
10. The helmsman moves to the centre of the boat, facing towards the stern, keeping his head down to avoid being hit by the boom, when it comes over.
11. Helmsman grasps the tiller with his free hand placing it behind the hand holding the tiller and mainsheet but NOT STRAIGHTENING THE TILLER.

12. Helmsman takes up the mainsheet in his 'front' hand.

13. During this change over, the boom will have moved over to the other side of the boat as the boat passes through the wind.

14. With the boom over, the helmsman has completed his move to the other side of the boat.

15. Helmsman waits until boat is COMPLETELY round on the new 'tack' and **then** straightens tiller.

16. Crew, having been balancing boat as she goes round, pulls on his 'new' jib sheet after the boat has passed through the wind. (It is always a tendency of the crew to pull on his 'new' sheet too early. Unless the jib is absolutely free whilst the boat is passing through the wind she will tend to 'stick' and may fall back on to the original tack.)

17. Finally the crew adjusts the centreboard, if it is necessary, to the new point of sailing.

Without doubt, going about in a competent fashion is the key to good sailing. It is really worthwhile to practise this manoeuvre on dry land and then to give yourself plenty of practice in calm conditions. It is quite surprising how long the tiller has to remain 'hard over' before the boat will come round, especially if you are going about from reach to reach which, as we have said before, is the safest point of sailing.

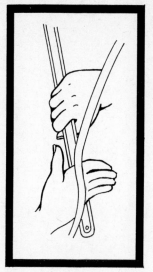

Handling the mainsheet while tacking is essentially a matter of practice. Having tacked, it is important to pick up the mainsheet, in the 'new' hand, in a smooth easy movement, which leaves you holding the mainsheet 'overhand' in the forward hand. The sheet leads above the hand holding the tiller and down into the bottom of the boat where it cannot be tangled, or caught up.

No-go Zone

It is vital to understand that, if you turn the boat towards the wind, without a definite intention of 'tacking' through the wind and changing direction, the boat will gradually slow up as it gets nearer and nearer to the wind and ultimately will go 'into irons'. (See Fig. 4 on Page 7 again.)

If you are intending to 'tack' and do not push the tiller AWAY from you and KEEP IT THERE, you will enter the No-Go Zone. Equally if you sail too close to the wind the same thing will happen.

Plate 4. There are several mistakes being made by this crew. The boat is 'heeled' too far over. They should adjust their weight and lean further out. The luff of the sail is bulging, therefore they are too close to the No-Go Zone. The helmsman should pull the tiller a little towards him. Note the gap at the foot of the mainsail between it and the mast. They have failed to ensure that the mainsail was fully hoisted.

A boat will sail with the wind, across the wind but not against the wind. Suppose that you are in Boat A in Fig. 11. You have got as close to the direction of the wind as you dare go when you are at position A1. If you sail even closer to the wind (A2), the boat will slow up. If you do not intend to turn and bring your boat to position A3 you must do something to get her sailing again. Of course, you pull the tiller **towards** you and your boat will turn off to position A4.

It will be clear that, if you are at A1 and wish to bring your boat into position A3, you will be best to be 'close-hauled' and then to tack. That will be the quickest way of turning—from close-hauled on the port tack to close hauled on the starboard tack. Note once again that the crew have changed position so that their backs are to the wind.

Signals of No-Go

What are the physical signs that you are in danger of straying into the 'No-Go Zone'?

If the wind is constant, the first sign will be that your boat begins to slow up and the jib luff will, in most boats, start 'shivering'. Indeed, it may start to fill with wind ON THE WRONG SIDE! Your mainsail will progressively start bulging the wrong way at about half-way up the luff. The burgee will start pointing closer over the stern. PULL THE TILLER TOWARDS YOU and all will be well.

Refinements of sail setting

The elementary positions of the sails have been discussed. 'Sheeted in', 'eased', etc. The actual steering of the boat has also been discussed. Too close to the wind, pull tiller towards you. To tack, push it away. These explanations simplify a little too much.

Clearly if you are sailing on a reach, with the sheets half let out, as you turn *towards* the wind, the sails will flap and you must sheet in the sail until it stops flapping. If the front edge (the luff) of either sail is flapping, it needs sheeting in, until it sets and is clearly utilising the wind to its best advantage. So the use of the rudder, the set of the sails and the body weight distribution are all important.

We will be discussing body weight distribution later but it is clear that you will not be anywhere near the No-Go Zone when sailing on a *reach* or a *run*.

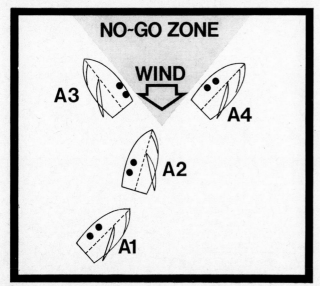

Fig. 11

Sailing down-wind

If you turn your boat to sail before the wind, it is important to watch the jib. Clearly, the mainsail will 'blanket' the jib, protecting it from the wind. The jib will start to hang limp and if you keep on pulling the tiller towards you, moving from a reach to a run, the jib will *start* to move to the other side of the boat. Straighten the tiller and keep the jib on the same side as the mainsail, preferably keeping it slightly 'drawing' (i.e., with **some** wind acting on it).

Getting from A to B

One of the more difficult parts of dinghy sailing is working out the best course to steer in order to arrive at a given destination. Sailing is NOT an aimless floating about being blown where the wind wishes to take you. The wind is your servant.

Fig. 12 overleaf shows the probable course of a boat when aiming at four different points on a lake.

To get to B from A, you cannot sail straight there because you will be sailing straight into the No-Go Zone. You have to tack back and forth. A to C is a simple reach. A to the church is a broad reach. The real trouble starts with A to D.

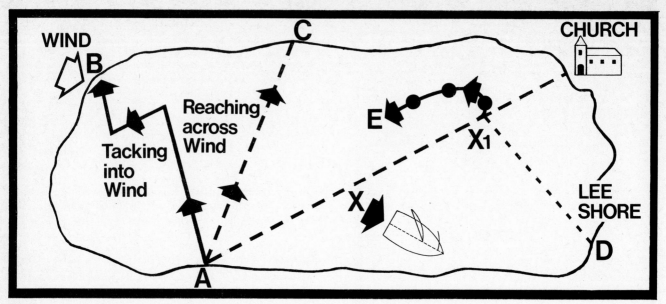

Fig. 12

You cannot sail along the shallow shore line. So, you must go out towards the church. If you turn at X, you will be sailing ABSOLUTELY down wind and, if the wind shifts just a little, it could go round the back of your sail and SLAM your boom over. It is therefore safer to travel as far as X1 and turn there, on to another broad reach. Have you realised that at X1 you will not be putting the bow of your boat through the wind? Oh! No! You will be turning the stern of your boat through the wind. This is known as 'gybing' and is explained on page 17. Before we discuss gybing however, consider trying to *tack* at X1. Turning the bow into the wind will eventually turn you on to Course E and unless you want to return to A, without reaching D, that course is clearly no good at all!

Controlled Gybing

In Fig. 12 we discussed the course to take from A to D and we said that you would have to gybe to do it. We have discussed sailing down-wind and *avoiding* a gybe. Here is the drill for a safe gybe. (See Fig. 13.)

1. Centreboard a quarter down.
2. Helmsman checks all round and calls 'stand by to gybe'.
3. Helmsman brings in his mainsail by hauling in on his mainsheet until the boom is about a foot from the side of the boat at the stern.
4. Helmsman holds mainsheet and tiller in one hand, and pulls the tiller towards him, calling 'Gybe oh!'
5. As the helmsman calls, the crew frees his jib sheet and prepares to haul in on the other. He also prepares to balance the boat.
6. With the boat turning its stern through the wind, the helmsman transfers the tiller to his 'free' hand, moves to the centre of the boat, KEEPING HIS HEAD DOWN, and as the boom swings across he straightens the tiller and sits down on the 'windy' side of the boat.
7. As the wind fills the mainsail, and starts causing a real 'pull' on the mainsheet, the helmsman lets the mainsheet out, a bit at a time, to keep the boat sailing hard. The crew-man sheets in the jib a little.

Later on, when you are really experienced at 'balancing' your boat, you may do this manoeuvre WITHOUT sheeting in the mainsail really at all. This is known as 'gybing all standing'. It is tough on the boat and its rigging and 'courts' a capsize, unless very experienced.

Chinese Gybe

By mistake, you will certainly get yourself into a gybing situation at some time. If you allow your boat to get into a position where the wind is blowing parallel to the boom (on to the end of the boom), the boat will tend to gybe. If you do not have your 'kicking strap' rigged to hold the boom down the boom will blow upwards and lie up the mast! This is known as a 'Chinese' gybe and is a very uncomfortable experience in a wobbling dinghy! Avoid it, by gybing intentionally and getting your boom on the side of the boat away from the wind.

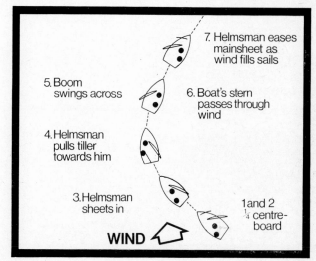

Fig. 13

Trimming the boat

Weight distribution is important to the fore and aft attitude of the boat. There are really four 'rules' which are illustrated in Fig. 14.

1. **When close-hauled,** most boats sail best with the crew weight slightly towards the bow. When close-hauled, the helmsman must ALWAYS sit clear of the arc of his tiller. Urgent alteration may be necessary!

2. **When reaching,** across the wind, the crew and helmsman will probably be on the same side of the boat, but whether they sit out depends on wind strength.

3. **When running,** before the wind, the 'uprightness' of the boat may best be achieved by the crew member sitting centrally in the boat, or even slightly to 'leeward'.

4. **When sailing down-wind,** both crew would be as far aft as possible. With centreboard nearly up, and the bow of the boat out of the water, she will 'plane' over the water. As a novice, this may be **too** exciting!

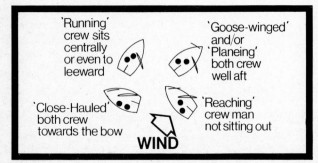

'Running' crew sits centrally or even to leeward

'Goose-winged' and/or 'Planeing' both crew well aft

'Close-Hauled' both crew towards the bow

'Reaching' crew man not sitting out

WIND

Fig. 14

This picture of a dinghy reaching across the wind gives a good idea of the way to balance a boat. The crew has remembered that the boat should be level and is sitting well out. His helmsman does not therefore need to, and can concentrate on sailing the boat from a comfortable position. Note how bulky the crew man looks. He is wearing his buoyancy aid underneath his oilskin. Note also the luff of the jib. Whilst rigging, this crew failed to tighten the jib halyard sufficiently.

RIGHTING AFTER CAPSIZE

Despite all your efforts your boat capsizes and you are thrown into the water. Both crew move to stern and check that the rudder is safely fixed and that the mainsheet is quite free and not likely to get tangled. Then the helmsman moves round to the centreboard and the crew ensures that it is down, so that the helmsman can put his arms over it. The crew then throws the jib sheet over the hull to the helmsman who should shout that he has got it.

The three illustrations on this page show the sequence of events. It is quite possible that the rudder WILL need re-fixing (without it you will be in trouble). It is VITAL to ensure that the mainsheet is free because, when you do right the boat, if the mainsheet holds the boom in, the sails will not 'weathercock', the mainsail will fill with wind and blow the boat over again. As soon as the helmsman has the jibsheet

Plate 6 (opposite). Both crew move to stern.
Plate 7 (above). Crew throws jib sheet to helmsman.
Plate 8 (below). Helmsman climbs on to centreboard.

in his hands, he climbs on the centreboard, CLOSE to the boat so that the board does not snap. The crew lies in the boat as illustrated and is scooped up as the helmsman's weight causes the boat to come upright. The helmsman will fall forward as the boat comes upright. In Plate 10, the crew is already moving to help his helms-*woman* aboard.

Complete inversion

It sometimes happens that the boat goes right over as in Plate 11. If you are trapped underneath, don't panic. There is an airpocket. Just get your breath, then 'duck dive' under and out, making sure not to get caught up in any of the ropes.

If the boat is fully inverted, it will be necessary to start your capsize drill by putting weight on one corner of the stern to 'break the vacuum'.

Plate 9 (opposite). Crew lies in boat.
Plate 10 (above). Helmsman starts righting boat.
Plate 11 (below). Put weight on corner to free 'vacuum'.

COMING ASHORE

At the end of your sail, or if you want to picnic, you will have to bring the boat into the shore. If you are approaching a shore on to which the wind is blowing, you will be running before the wind, and going far too fast for comfort. It is best to turn up into the wind, some way off the shore, lower your mainsail, and then turn and run before the wind towards the shore, using your jib only. As you near the shore you can let the jib sheet out (and in) just so that you nicely judge your arrival. As you approach, you will have to raise your centreboard and, finally, the rudder.

Approaching a shore when the wind is blowing towards you from the shore (a weather shore), you can, of course, judge your tacks so that you eventually arrive sailing across the wind, then let your sails weathercock and pull up the centreboard and rudder as your arrive.

If your trolley is nearby, roll it into the water and float the boat on to it. Do not drag the boat on to the trolley. You may do a lot of damage. Just float it neatly on, see that it is central and firm and then walk the trolley out of the water.

If you are on a shore where there is no trolley, it may be necessary to lift the boat and carry it up the beach. Don't drag it, unless you HAVE to. Again, you can cause a lot of damage.

ANCHORING

It is more usual for a dinghy to be brought ashore than to be anchored in deep water. However, it may be necessary to anchor in deep water at some time, so you should have a good dinghy anchor (one with folding 'blades' held by a ring is very handy and will not damage your boat). The anchor should have a good long length of, preferably, nylon rope attached to it AND to the boat. Don't forget, if you come ashore in tidal waters, the tide may be rising. You should check what it is doing. If it is rising, lay out your anchor rope well up the beach, and dig the anchor well in, preferably burying it completely, so that anybody walking along the beach cannot stumble over the very sharp 'blades' (correctly called *flukes*). A one-foot rise of tide, may bring the sea ten or twelve feet up a shelving beach, so see to it that you lay out plenty of rope.

If the tide is ebbing, then you have to realise that your boat may eventually be 'stranded' miles from the water. If it is heavy, or you are weak, it can be hard work getting afloat again. So, if the tide is ebbing, leave your dinghy afloat, and anchor it PROPERLY some way off the beach, and wade ashore. Then, when you are ready, your boat may still be afloat or just at the edge of the sea.

At all times, remember to ensure that your anchor rope is securely fastened to your dinghy. It is purposeless to lay out an anchor which is not attached to your boat!

SAFETY AT SEA

This section of Know the Game Sailing is, from the point of view of your family, the most important part of the book. Whether you are somebody's son or daughter, mother or father or close friend, you must realise that your life is at risk, unless you take precautions.

Personal Equipment

Sailing clothing (oilskins etc.) is always brightly coloured. You may have thought it was merely a fad of the manufacturers. It is not. The most distinctive colours should always be worn, preferably orange, since it stands out well against water. You will seldom find a *blue* lifejacket. Buy a lifejacket or, at the least, a personal buoyancy aid (which, as we have said, has less buoyancy in it). Buy yourself really warm and waterproof clothing. Cold can kill and with all that wind and water, you can get cold even on a sunny day.

Man overboard

In a modern two-man dinghy, the likelihood of capsize if one member of the crew goes overboard is quite great. However, on occasions, especially if it is the helmsman who is left in the boat, there is a good chance that the situation can be remedied without capsize.

As soon as a member of the crew goes overboard, his position should be marked and the remaining crew should put the boat on to a reach (sailing across the wind).

After as short a time as possible to get organised, the boat should be tacked on to the (reciprocal) course back towards

the person in the water, and it should be sailed so as to approach the person from down-wind.

The head of a person in the water is a very small object and you should at all times try to keep a very sharp eye on the 'victim'.

Practice in the man overboard situation should form part of your early sailing. Apart from anything else, approaching a mooring or a man in the water are rather similar activities.

As the man is approached, the sheets should be let go. The sails will 'weathercock' and the boat should stop so that the man is alongside the weather shrouds. For a variety of reasons it is not easy to recover somebody from the water over the stern.

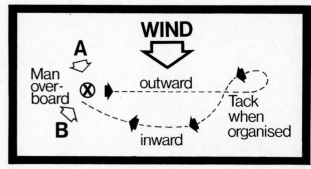

Fig. 15. Man overboard. Whatever point of sailing you are on, as soon as the man goes over, turn on to a reach, get organised and return towards him, approaching from downwind. On course A, running before the wind, it is easy to sheet in and turn on to a reach. From course B, close hauled, it is easy to ease sheets and turn on to the same reach.

Having let go of everything, the helmsman moves to the shrouds. In really boisterous conditions the boat may heel over as the man is brought aboard. If it capsizes, go through the capsize drill (pages 19 and 20).

Plate 12. The man overboard is recovered from the windward side, close to the centre of the boat. The sails are 'blowing away' to leeward and are therefore kept out of the way.

CURRENTS AND TIDAL STREAMS

Sometime in your life you have, no doubt, thrown a stick into a stream, and watched it float down on the current, waiting for it to be caught in an eddy, or hurried along by the main stream.

Throw your dinghy in the river and you will find that it floats down, etc., etc! You will, with difficulty be able to sail against the current, and, with the greatest of ease, with it. Going with it you will travel far and fast, with wind and water both helping.

Translate this example to the seashore. We all know that the tides go out and come in, they 'ebb' and they 'flow'. From the start of an 'ebb' to the time when the tide turns and starts to flood in again is approximately six hours. Whilst it is doing this, all that water further out is going somewhere, and FAST.

If the tide, as an example, is on this particular day, going to rise twelve feet from its lowest point, it will do so slowly at first, very fast in the middle of its time and more slowly near the end of its rise. One foot in the first hour, two in the second, three in the third and fourth, two in the fifth, and one in the last. 1-2-3-3-2-1. Hence in the third and fourth hours the actual tidal streams will be flowing very fast.

This is why commercial ships sail 'with the tide'. It costs less in fuel to be floated along than to butt against the tide. For the same effort with the tide, they will travel far further than against it.

You may say that you knew all this. Many do not and,

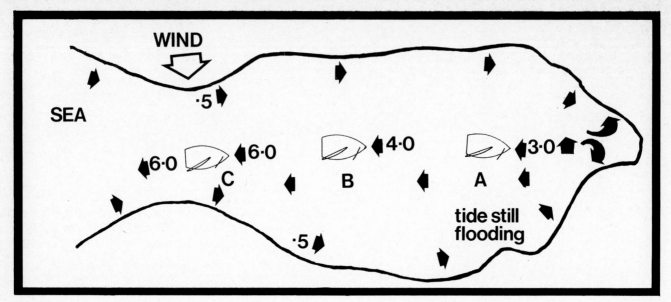

Fig. 16

when you are in a sailing boat, for some reason the action of the tide is not readily apparent.

In Fig. 16 we have imagined that the tide has started to ebb. We have indicated each arrow in 'knots'—nautical miles per hour—(we never talk of knots per hour).

Suppose your boat, with the *present* strength of the wind, would do 5 knots in still water. At point A you would clearly be only travelling forward at 2 knots. At point B at 1 knot, and at point C you will actually be going backwards, whilst *apparently* sailing like mad with your sails all working hard! And *that* is the danger. If you are trying to get back to the shore, which you so gaily left 'on the tide', and the tide has turned against you, it will take a long time to get home.

Furthermore, if the wind is blowing in the direction of the tide, the sea will be comparatively smooth. If during the course of the afternoon, the tide changes and the wind remains constant, the water will get *much* rougher.

Strong wind against strong tide
You're in for a rough ride.

Perhaps the most interesting part of Fig. 16 is the indication that if you do want to get home, against the tide, the 'bath plug effect' is that the water along the very edges of the banks is PROBABLY still going your way, or at the worst, is 'slack' or still. Tide-dodging is a favourite trick and one way of winning races. However, this effect depends entirely upon the state of the tide. All that water has eventually to flow away, before the tide starts to flood back into our creek.

Indications of tidal conditions

In every place, and on every day, the tides are different. A local yachting shop will usually have a card showing the tides for the whole year, so will the Harbour master, the Coastguard and most of the local population who use boats. It is vital knowledge to them, AND to you.

Even if you have not got this information, there are many indications of what the tide is doing. Boats at moorings will almost invariably face the flow of the tide, lie across it when it is 'slack', and turn to face it when it changes. Buoys will have a build-up of water on one side, so will the supports of jetties. Even an examination of the shore-line will give an indication. If it is nearly dry, the tide has clearly gone down (been ebbing) for some time.

Indications of weather to come

Once having established, from the many national forecasts what the general weather pattern is to be, there is a definite daily sequence of weather pattern in summer weather away from depressions. The formation of sea breezes usually builds up from about eleven in the morning and reaches maximum in the early afternoon. These 'local' sea breezes can modify the winds from the major weather systems and vary from place to place. Frankly, as a dinghy sailor, although it is useful to listen to the shipping forecasts, they are not so useful as the Post Office telephones local forecasts and, even better, the many places round the country from which you can get a report by phone of the *immediate* probabilities FOR THE LOCALITY.

Coastguard stations, lighthouses, Signal Stations and the Harbour Master's Office, and possibly the local R.A.F. station will all provide local knowledge. If you are a stranger to the area, the weather is not the only 'hazard' about which the local people will tell you, if you ask.

There is much to learn about taking your boat to a likely looking beach, and launching it.

Hidden Dangers

There is a little red flag flying over there! It could be to stop bathers. It actually tells you that firing is in progress on the local firing range and that there is a possibility that bullets or shells may land in the Sea Danger Area which isn't buoyed all round and into which you are about to launch! Even dangerous currents may not be immediately visible or threatening so DO find out before launching.

BUOYS AND BUOYAGE SYSTEMS

Dinghy sailing is essentially a day-time sport and one which, wherever possible, should be conducted outside the main shipping channels. It is, however, important for even the smallest ship's skipper to know something about the signposts of the sea.

Navigation channels are marked for ships which are coming in from the sea, on the flood tide.

The left hand (port) side of the channel is marked with RED can-shaped buoys and the right hand side by BLACK conical buoys. They may be chequered red and white or black and white, but the predominant colour is red or black as the case may be.

If there is an obstacle, like a sudden bank, in the middle of the channel, then it will be marked with round horizontally striped buoys, either red and white or black and white, indicating which is the *preferable* side to leave them on.

In Fig. 17 a big ship would take Route A. In a cruising yacht, the helmsman might well take route B keeping in the less important channel.

In a dinghy, you can keep outside the buoys altogether because it will be safer, and if you do run aground, you can pull up the centre-board.

In even narrower rivers, not used by commercial navigation, you may well find only sticks indicating the edges of the deep water channel.

There are other sorts of buoys, including a 'wreck' buoy which will be green, with the word 'wreck' on it. It may be can-shaped, conical or spherical and its shape indicates again which side you should leave it.

Never sail too close to a buoy, the tide may sweep you on to it, and it is stronger than your boat.

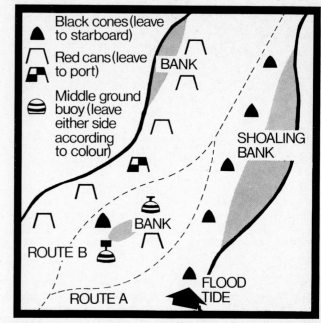

Fig. 17. The lateral buoyage system. The middle ground buoys, marking the bank, are red and white, therefore, for preference, a large ship would take route A and then keep to the right hand of the channel.

RULES OF THE ROAD

Having discussed the signposts of the sea, it must be clear that there is also some system to avoid any chance of collision, since there are no roads on the sea, and no white lines.

Vessels in any channel normally keep to the right, if the depth allows them to do so.

There are three rules about sailing vessels meeting.

When each has the wind on a different side, the vessel which has the wind on the PORT side shall keep out of the way of the other. So a sailing vessel which is on the Starboard Tack has priority and the others must keep out of the way. Look at Fig. 18 and decide which vessel has priority. (Answer on Page 28).

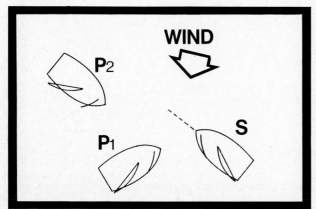

Fig. 18

Next—'When both have the wind on the same side, the vessel which is to windward shall keep out of the way of the vessel which is to leeward. Which of the dinghies in Plate 13 has priority? Think where the wind is coming from. (Answer on Page 28).

Plate 13

The third rule for sailing vessels (and for power vessels) is 'An overtaking vessel shall keep clear'.

Another important rule is 'Power gives way to sail'.

However, do not expect a big commercial craft to turn aside for your small dinghy, especially in a narrow channel.

We have deliberately simplified the rules as much as possible. The full text is contained in 'The International Regulations for the Prevention of Collisions at Sea'. WHATEVER THE ACTUAL RULES SAY there is a general duty on all mariners to avoid collision. So, you avoid getting in the way of commercial ships, and, if you are going to change course, do it FIRMLY, BOLDLY, and in AMPLE TIME so that your intentions are clear. Remember also, that the wind may die away quite suddenly so do not leave yourself in a position where you are in danger, or likely to be a danger to others because you suddenly get becalmed.

Answers to questions on Page 27

In Fig. 18, vessel S has priority because she is on the starboard tack.

In Plate 13, the left hand vessel is nearer the wind (she is the windward vessel) and therefore must keep out of the way of the other.

Now look at Fig. 19. We agreed that S has priority, but what do P1 and P2 do? P2 is nearer the wind than P1 and both are on the port tack. P2 must keep out of the way of P1. She must also keep out of the way of S. This may resolve itself like this:—

1. S carries on, not altering course.
2. P1 alters course to pass under the stern of S.
3. P2 could either ease sheets and run before the wind or,

IF SHE IS SURE SHE HAS SPACE AND TIME, sheet in and hurry across S's course.

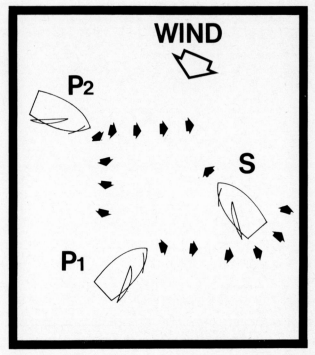

Fig. 19

KNOTS, BENDS AND HITCHES

It is not possible to teach you all the knots in a book of this length but merely to illustrate them and explain their uses. In the first place, bends are knots used to tie the end of two *free* lines together. A hitch is a knot used to secure a line to a spar, ring or post and a knot is any other type.

An efficient knot must be easily and quickly tied, become more secure as the strain on it increases and be untied easily, even when wet. The main part of the rope is called the standing part—a loop is called a bight and the end of the rope, the free or running end.

Half Hitch

This is the simplest form of knot and the basis of many others, It is, by itself, a very temporary fastening.

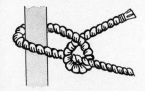

Fig. 20

Figure of eight

A simple knot used to stop the end of any rope running through a block etc.

Fig. 21

Slippery Hitch

Fig. 22

This hitch is used for the temporary securing of a rope. It is illustrated here on a cleat but could just as well be tied around a thwart, through a ring or round a bollard.

Cleating a sheet

This is NOT a knot. Lead sheet round A, then round B and then wind on in a figure of eight as illustrated. Sheets should never be made fast (i.e., locked on to a cleat). They must be easy and quick to undo, even when wet.

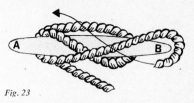

Fig. 23

Reef knot

Fig. 24

The reef knot is used for tying the two ends of a single rope together. For example, to put a tie round a sail. It should not be used for tying *two* ropes together and will 'spill' if one end is pulled sharply upwards.

29

The Bowline

Used to tie a fixed loop in the end of a rope. It is simple and strong, and does not slip or jam even when wet. Tie up your dinghy with this knot and it will not float away on the tide. Tie two lengths of rope together, with a bowline in the end of each, in order to make a long length of rope.

Fig. 25

Sheet Bend

Fig. 26

Tied in the same way as a bowline and used for tying two ropes of a similar diameter together, or for attaching a rope to a loop.

Double Sheet Bend

This is the best method of joining two ropes of unequal diameter. Very useful for tying your bow rope (painter) to a towing line or for attaching a rope to an eye-splice or ring.

Fig. 27

Rolling or stopper hitch

Fig. 28

For attaching to a tow-line, or for holding fast another rope. Wrap round once, then again, jamming the second turn inside the first. Finish with a half-hitch. Works very well when the strain is parallel, or near parallel to the axis of the larger rope.

Clove Hitch

A simple 'cross' hitch for attaching a rope to a spar or post.

Fig. 29

Round Turn and Two Half Hitches

Fig. 30

Used for making fast the boat's painter or other rope to a post or ring. The Hitches both go the SAME way.

Other knots

There are many hundreds of other knots, all with their different uses. For the average dinghy sailor, however, the knots described on the preceding pages are perhaps the most commonly used.

There is, for example, the Fisherman's or Anchor Bend which is nothing more than a round turn and two half-hitches with the first half-hitch passed through the round turn. This is a very strong, non-slip, non-jamming knot which is useful when securing your anchor to its line. Every knot has its special use to a competent sailor.

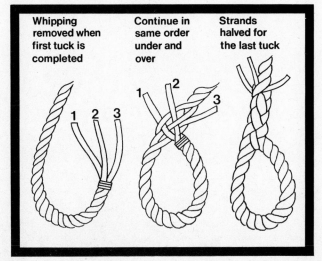

Whipping removed when first tuck is completed

Continue in same order under and over

Strands halved for the last tuck

1 2 3

Fig. 31

SPLICING

The illustration on this page is of the various stages of an Eye Splice. A splice is stronger, neater and more permanent than a knot. An Eye Splice can be used for permanent attachment of your painter to the boat, for fenders etc. Splicing two pieces of rope together is a similar operation.

With modern synthetic ropes, which are quite 'slippery' to the touch, the first thing to do is to whip the rope about nine inches from its end. This stops the whole rope unravelling. As soon as you have 'unlayed' the rope, weld the individual ends by heating them, wet your fingers and roll each strand together. This will stop the smaller strands of each strand 'fraying'.

Tuck the middle strand (strand 1) under one strand of the rope, at the required position. Tuck strand 2 under the next-door strand. Then turn the work over and tuck strand 3 under the remaining adjacent strand. It is important not to get into a muddle at the start. All three strands must be tucked in at the same point longitudinally along the rope. The following tucks will then come naturally.

It is usually sufficient to tuck each strand three times, even with synthetic rope. For the last tuck, the strand can be halved so that the splice tapers in neatly. Do not cut off the ends too close because they may work out when the rope is under strain.

If you are very careful not to apply too much heat, it is possible to melt the ends of a splice in synthetic rope to get a good finish. Be careful not to weaken the whole job by over-heating.

WHIPPINGS

There are, in fact, five kinds of whippings but the most usual are illustrated on this page. Although the modern synthetic ropes can be layed together, heated and the strands will hold together, there may be some occasions when it is necessary to whip a rope end to stop it unravelling.

The Common Whipping

All whippings, whatever kind, should be done with suitable size waxed seizing twine which can be bought on reels and is very easy to work.

Lay a piece of twine along the rope near the end, then wind on half a dozen turns, close to each other, not overlapping. Then lay the piece which you are holding in a loop as illustrated and go on turning. Finally haul both ends up taut (they will be in the middle of the whipping) and cut them off short.

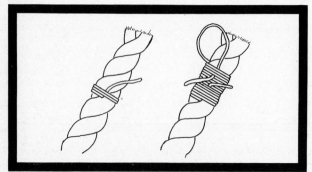

Fig. 32

The Sailmaker's whipping

Pass the loop of twine through the rope as illustrated. Leave one end and wind on the other up the rope. Then lift the loop (correctly called a 'bight') drop it over the end of its original strand, bring both ends together (tightly) and tie in a reef knot concealed in the ends of the strands.

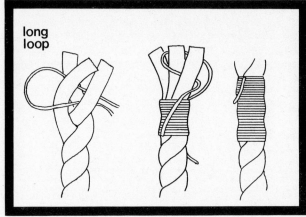

long loop

Fig. 33

The West Country whipping

'Middle' a piece of twine on the rope and half-knot it at each turn. After a dozen turns, finish with a reef knot. This is quite a convenient whipping when the end is short or the rope is awkwardly placed.

WHO MAKES THE RACING RULES?

In every sport, there are rules which have been thought out over the years by those taking part. In every country there is a National Authority for yacht racing. In the United Kingdom this is one of the many functions of the Royal Yachting Association. It, in turn, is one of sixty-three member organisations which go to make up the International Yacht Racing Union, which is the world-wide body and makes the rules, to which each country then adds its own prescriptions according to its particular needs.

All the rules and prescriptions are contained in the R.Y.A. Booklet YR1. The words in this book which are printed in bold type are defined precisely in that booklet.

In this book, we only deal with the main rules. These are to ensure that collisions are avoided and to indicate which yacht has to keep clear and, by inference, which yacht has the right of way. The racing rules start to apply when a yacht is in the vicinity of the starting line.

The first universal rule is that when two sailing vessels on opposite tacks meet, the vessel on the **port tack** must keep clear of the vessel on the **starboard tack** (Fig. 34(a)).

In Fig. 34(b) if you are in vessel A, the vessel L is said to be to leeward (pronounced lu-ard) of you, and the vessel W is to windward. The International Regulations for the Prevention of Collisions at Sea (the law followed by ALL ships, whether racing or not) says that when vessels have the wind on the same side, the vessel which is to **windward** shall keep out of the way of a vessel to **leeward.** As far as racing is

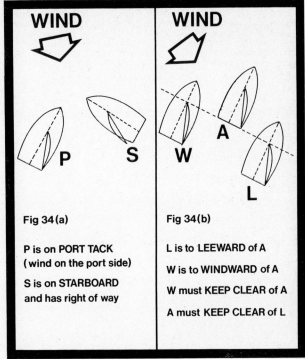

Fig. 34(a)

P is on PORT TACK (wind on the port side)

S is on STARBOARD and has right of way

Fig. 34(b)

L is to LEEWARD of A

W is to WINDWARD of A

W must KEEP CLEAR of A

A must KEEP CLEAR of L

Fig. 34

concerned, W must keep clear of A, and A must keep clear of L, when the vessels are **overlapping** and are on the same **tack.**

Fig 35		Fig 36 (a)	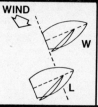	Fig 36 (b)	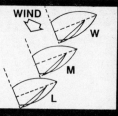
W is CLEAR AHEAD of L. L is CLEAR ASTERN of W. If L is gaining on W, she is the overtaking yacht clear astern, until OVERLAP is established		An OVERLAP has been established between W and L and W (being WINDWARD YACHT) must keep clear		M connects W and L and OVERLAP therefore exists between W and L	

OVERTAKING

When a vessel is overtaking another, she must, you remember, keep clear. During racing, this duty continues until an **overlap** has been established. Figs. 35 and 36 explain **overlap.**

Then there is what might be described as an 'intervening' **overlap.** In Fig. 36(b) an **overlap** exists between W and L. M **overlaps** each of them, and continues the 'joining up' process.

GOING RACING?

Unless you have been very well taught, you will spend time mastering all the technicalities of starting in a race.

In the following pages you will find the major points to watch.

You should first ensure that you have read the Sailing Instructions issued by the club. These may be agreed for the season, but there may also be special Instructions for the day.

Once you have broken a rule, you cannot always put it right, and may have to retire, be penalised or disqualified.

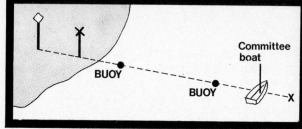

Fig. 37

THE STARTING LINE

The starting line is usually indicated by a post or posts on the shore, or by marker buoys, or by the mast of a Committee boat. When all are in line, they form a 'transit'—an imaginary line drawn between them. All boats starting in a race must cross the starting line, after the starting signal has been made, between the marks showing the limits of the starting line. In Fig. 37 you would not **start** by crossing at point X.

OVER THE LINE

A yacht **starts** when, after the starting signal, any part of her hull, crew or equipment (unless otherwise prescribed in the sailing instructions) first crosses the starting line in the direction of the first **mark.** A yacht on the course side of the line at the start will be recalled by a sound signal, probably a bell or a gun, and, quite often, the Race Committee will display the yacht's number. This is often difficult, and more usually, after one sound signal, the class warning signal is brought 'to the dip' (i.e., half way down the mast) until all premature starters are wholly on the pre-start side of the starting line. It is the responsibility of all premature starters to return and re-start.

When a number of premature starters are over the starting line, race officers have an impossible task and will probably order a **double** sound signal to be made and the 'General Recall' signal to be broken out on the flag mast.

Usually, the flags used are those of the International Code and the 'General Recall' is the 'First Substitute'. It is a triangular flag with a blue border and a yellow middle. (Fig. 38).

FLAGS AT THE START

Ten minutes before the start of a race, the race officers will break out your particular class flag. Five minutes before the start, Flag P will be broken out. (This is a rectangular flag bordered in blue with a white rectangular panel in the centre). It is almost universally used as the Preparatory signal. (Fig.38).

When it is the turn of your class to start, both flags will be lowered. Attention is drawn to all these signals by the firing of a gun, blowing of a whistle or other sound.

You can guarantee that if you are in a large fleet, and therefore some distance from the shore, the sound will reach you well after the signal has been made. It pays to 'count down' from the ten minute warning signal with an efficient stop watch.

PREMATURE STARTERS

In case it is not quite clear, you get one gun at the ten minute warning time, one gun at the five minute (when the Blue Peter is broken out) and **a gun at the start.** THEN, if there is **one** yacht over the line an immediate second gun, and if there is a crowd over the line, **two** guns will be fired. Fig. 39 shows the three flag signals which we have described as they will appear on the club flagstaff.

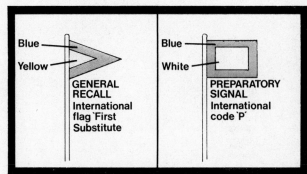

Blue — Yellow — **GENERAL RECALL International flag 'First Substitute'**

Blue — White — **PREPARATORY SIGNAL International code 'P'**

Fig. 38

THE ACTUAL START

Fig. 40 shows an imaginary situation which explains much of what has been described about starting procedures. Boat G is over the line and MUST keep clear of any boats which are starting correctly, whether they are on the **port** or **starboard tack.** She is an outsider, an outcast and has no rights in the race until she is wholly on the pre-start side of the starting line.

Looking at the other boats, P must keep clear of S (port tack vessel keeps clear).

An overtaking boat must keep clear when overtaking to windward, so W must keep clear of L. If L chooses to **luff** (turn slightly up into the wind) W, the **windward yacht,** must keep out of the way but L must only luff slowly so that W can respond if this situation develops between the preparatory (five minute signal) and the starting signal.

If X were a turning **mark** of the course, and not a

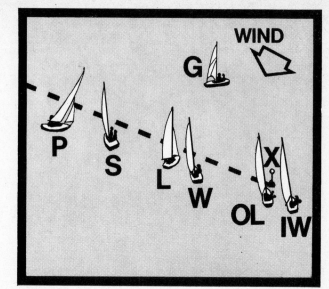

Fig. 40

starting **mark,** OL would have to give room for IW to pass between her and the **mark.** However, OL is making a good start on the **starboard tack** at the windward end of the line and does not on this occasion have to give IW room.

AFTER THE STARTING SIGNAL, a **leeward yacht** must not deprive a **windward yacht** of room at a starting **mark** by sailing either above the course to the first **mark** or above 'close-hauled'.

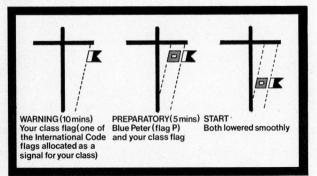

WARNING (10 mins)
Your class flag (one of the International Code flags allocated as a signal for your class)

PREPARATORY (5 mins)
Blue Peter (flag P) and your class flag

START ·
Both lowered smoothly

Fig. 39

DURING THE RACE

After clearing the starting line, if conditions permit the **leeward yacht** to **luff** she may do so. Yachts W and L in Fig. 41 illustrate what is meant by luffing. L is forcing W to change course, which is racing tactics which we will discuss more fully later.

A yacht which does not observe a rule which requires her to keep clear can be disqualified whether a collision has resulted or not. Sometimes the sailing instructions will prescribe some other penalty rather than disqualification.

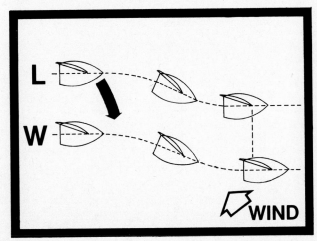

Fig. 41

PROTESTS

During a race, if you feel that you have a right to protest against another yacht for an infringement of the rules, you should hoist a white flag (tying a handkerchief in the rigging will do!). You should inform her that you intend to protest when you have finished the race and, when ashore, fill in a protest form, stating the names of the boats, describing what happened and when. You must also quote the rule which you believe was infringed. This form must be lodged with the race committee. You will be told when your protest will be heard.

If a yacht which has the right-of-way has to alter course to avoid a collision, she should immediately protest. A right-of-way yacht is herself under a duty to avoid collision. If she made no reasonable attempt to avoid it she may also be disqualified. It is clearly sensible to hail the other yacht if you have right-of-way and there looks as if there is danger of collision. What you must not do is to stand on your rights until it is too late to avoid a collision.

If a yacht continues in a race, even although protests have been made against her, all other competitors must treat her as still taking part in the race and observe all the rules with respect to her. The reason for this rule is that she may turn out to be in the right!

ROUNDING A MARK OF THE COURSE

Having started your race round the course, let us see what rules will come into operation as you sail around.

At or near the first **mark** there is likely to be a cluster of yachts all jockeying to round it.

If two yachts **overlap** when they come within two overall lengths of the **mark,** the outside yacht must give room at the **mark** to the inside yacht, but the yacht **clear astern** must establish her **overlap** BEFORE the yacht **clear ahead** is WITHIN TWO OVERALL LENGTHS OF THE MARK. The yacht **clear ahead** does not need to give room UNTIL AN **OVERLAP** IS ESTABLISHED (and proved by the inside yacht).

However, even a yacht **clear ahead** may only **tack** (to round the **mark**) when she can clear the **yacht astern.** (Fig. 42).

An outside yacht to **leeward,** which already has the right to **luff,** may **luff** an inside **windward yacht** to the wrong side of the **mark** (but she must also pass the mark on the wrong side herself!).

Fig. 43

FOULING A MARK

As you reach the **mark,** you should remember that a **mark** can be fouled (touched) if the crew sitting outboard touches any part of it. You are part of your boat, so watch out! (Fig. 43).

The rule states that a yacht which touches a **mark** must either retire immediately, protest against another yacht for wrongfully forcing her to touch it, or exonerate herself by completing the rounding or passing of that **mark** and then re-rounding or re-passing it, as required to sail the course, without touching it.

OBSTRUCTIONS ON THE COURSE

Now we come to discussing **obstructions** to searoom. These are defined as any object that requires the yacht in danger of fouling it to make an immediate and substantial alteration of course to avoid it.

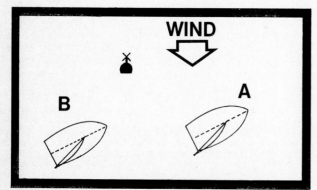

Fig. 42

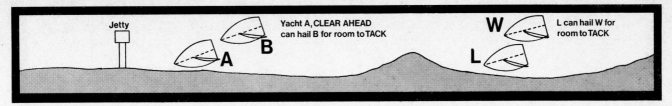

Fig. 44

Obstructions to searoom can, therefore, be of many kinds but quite the commonest is a large lump of land, especially if you race in inland or sheltered waters.

Fig. 44 illustrates the next rule. If two **overlapping** yachts are **close-hauled** on the same **tack** approaching an **obstruction**, and the **leeward yacht** must tack to clear it (and cannot do so without collision) she can hail the **windward yacht** for room to **tack,** which must be given. She must NOT hail and **tack** simultaneously.

Similarly, a yacht **clear ahead** which cannot tack without risk of collision with another yacht has a similar right to hail for room. (A and B in Fig. 44)

MARK OF THE COURSE

If the obstruction to sea room is a **mark** of the course, the yacht to **leeward** may not hail for room to **tack,** if the yacht to **windward** can 'fetch' the mark. In Fig. 45 yacht W can clearly reach the mark without tacking. L cannot therefore call for room to tack.

A **mark** is any object specified in the sailing instructions which a yacht must round or pass on a required side. It may be a club or navigational buoy, a lightship or a mark vessel.

TACTICS DURING RACING

We have already said that a yacht on the **port tack** must keep clear of a yacht on the **starboard tack**: That an **overtaking yacht** must keep clear and that a **windward yacht** must keep clear of a **leeward yacht.** If a yacht is overtaking to **leeward** of another yacht, she must allow the **windward yacht** room and opportunity to keep clear.

A yacht **tacking** or **gybing** must keep clear of one **on a tack** (i.e., starting to turn on to the other **tack**). If a yacht is

Fig 45

tacking or gybing into a position which will give her right-of-way, she must complete her **tack** or **gybe** far enough away from a yacht **on a tack** to enable the latter to hold her course until the **tack** or **gybe** is completed. If two yachts **tack** or **gybe** at the same time, the one on the other's **port** side must keep clear.

LUFFING OR BEARING AWAY

We have already briefly indicated that a little bit of games-manship can result in diverting another competitor from the course which he wishes to steer. However, even this 'game' is governed by very careful rules otherwise the sport would turn into a free-for-all.

When yachts are on the same **tack** a yacht may **luff** a yacht **clear astern** or a **windward yacht,** until the helmsman of the **windward yacht** comes abreast of the mainmast of the **leeward yacht.** The **leeward yacht** must not then sail above her **proper course** while that overlap continues to exist.

(Yachts must be within two yacht lengths of each other. The **windward yacht** must hail the **leeward yacht** when 'mast abeam'.) A yacht may **luff** only when she is in the correct position with respect to all yachts likely to be affected.

There are some conditions under which the **leeward yacht** may NOT luff and these are contained in Rule 38 of the I.Y.R.U. racing rules.

Fig. 41 showed an illustration of two yachts engaged in a luffing match. Equally a yacht on a free leg of the course shall not sail BELOW her proper course when within three lengths of a **leeward yacht** or of a yacht **clear astern** intending to pass to **leeward.** (Fig. 46).

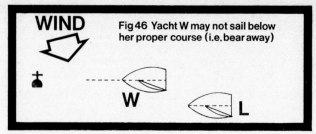

Fig 46 Yacht W may not sail below her proper course (i.e. bear away)

Fig. 46

ALTERING COURSE

When one yacht has to keep clear of another, the right of way yacht must not alter course to prevent her doing so or obstruct the other while she is keeping out of the way.

FINISHING

The finishing line is usually laid in the same way as was described for the starting line.

A yacht **finishes** when any part of her hull, or of her crew or equipment in normal position, crosses the finishing line from the direction of the last turning or guide **mark,** but she remains amenable to the racing rules until she has cleared the finishing line.

MANY MORE RULES

As we said earlier, there are many rules of this game of racing in sailing boats. If you know them you will enjoy your sport. If you break them, either intentionally or unintentionally, the sport is the poorer for it.

Printed in England by The White Rose Press, Mexborough and London.